THE OLD PUN

UNIVERSITY

PRESENTS

The Old Pun University Book of Uncommon Knowledge

Compiled by Graham Fifield.

Cover Design by Sophie Evans.

Illustrations by Alun Brown and Sophie Evans.

First published 2014

ISBN-13: 978-1502797179

ISBN-10: 1502797178

For their part in bringing this project to fruition thanks are due, to my wife for her patience and resolve, to Mrs Brown and her girls for their enthusiasm and encouragement and in particular to Sophie Evans and Alun Brown for much more than just their practical drawing and design contribution.

INTRODUCTION

"Punning is a talent which no man effects to despise but he that is without it" ... **Jonathan Swift**

"Puns are the highest form of literature" ... **Alfred Hitchcock**

"I like nonsense ...it wakes up the brain cells" ... **Dr Seuss**

The pun is a powerful tool in the armoury of the stand-up comedian or humourist, enabling the latter in particular to change details of events in history, the names and plots of films, books, famous poems and quotations. The list is seemingly endless. The vast majority of puns are either homophonic (based on using word pairings that sound the same but have totally different meanings) or homographic (pairs of words spelled the same but having totally different meanings) but it is the ability to use combinations or variation that is the mark of the great 'pundit'. ET, for example was a homophonic expert. Even so, reactions may vary tremendously and what satisfaction does the 'pundit' derive from the blank face of incomprehension? Better the groan than the silence; better the titter than the groan; better the laugh than the titter.

The Old Pun University is dedicated to raising awareness and true understanding of the pun and is therefore committed to its use in the teaching of all subjects irrespective of their inclusion or otherwise in the core curriculum. It is staffed by 'ex-pundits', heads of now diminished Faculties who have chosen to remain with the OPU in these difficult times, when changes in communication technology threaten the future of the English language as we know it today. These are men who have dealt with big issues in the past but would have no appetite for dealing with those words were they to appear in parentheses in this sentence, and be sold on street corners.

Our OPU shared nightmare scenario is the dinner party of the future where individual communication pads form part of the table setting and jokes are relayed around to hearty acknowledgements of LOL flashing on digital screens. As part of our programme we have therefore taken the decision to publish our archives in a series of books aimed at raising the profile of the pun in general, and particularly in the eyes of those who will produce future generations. Any parent reading this introduction before purchasing should ask themselves which of these they would prefer their child to become; a millionaire computer geek with the personality of an ironing board or an erudite, out of work bum who could charm the underwear off a convent washing line with a witty aside? On second thoughts read The Old Pun University Book of Uncommon Knowledge and let the kids decide for themselves.

Realising that age, culture and nationality can form barriers to true understanding we have taken the liberty of including footnotes as a pointer to further research that the reader may or may not wish to pursue. The alternative is to ask someone else in your family or community if they have any inkling as to what is going on. As academics we suggest the former, as pragmatists, the latter.

Volume I, of what is intended to be an extended series covering a range of University course subjects, begins by focussing on Media and the Arts with facts jokingly prepared on language, literature, cinema, art, music and poetry with the occasional scientific fact thrown in for good measure . It is a book of stark contrasts, ranging in format from introductory one-liner jokes to absurd pen pictures of historical characters interspersed with both historical and 'up to the minute' 'Breaking News' items, and quizzes and games designed to simultaneously test and insult the intelligence of the reader.

A compendium of nonsense for the thinking person, we give you, following payment of the appropriate fee, The Old Pun University Book of Uncommon Knowledge, Volume I.

Professor Plum with the Candlestick in the Library

Head of Diminished Faculties and Secretary (OPU)

(Unpaid electricity bill)

November, 2014.

PS. Though certain statements made within this book may appear to be valid, we would advise you to adopt what we refer to as 'the Lot approach' and take everything you read with a pinch of salt.

JOKES

I took my wife to a French restaurant last week. As we sat down so a waiter drove up to the next table in a motorised Cadbury's Drinking Chocolate Container and said "Ok, who ordered the Cocoa Van?"

To start, my wife ordered a plate of the parasitic skin disease that affects dogs and domestic fowl. I couldn't see anything else to tempt me, so I decided to have the mange tout.

For my main course I had a Himalayan Long-Haired Bovid stuffed with crisp stalks of a salad vegetable. It was the best Celery Yak I'd ever tasted.

While chatting, I asked my wife why a photograph of an old gypsy woman kept appearing on my lap top screen. She said "The cursor's most probably stuck again."

She recently went on a two day shopping trip to Switzerland but was diverted by the airline to Kenya. Even then she still managed to come back with a Kikuyu clock.

So the Colour Sergeant of the Welsh Guards had just taken to the dance floor at the annual Regimental dance when a glamorous blonde whispered in his ear "Get your goat, you've pulled."

I was standing on the tube yesterday morning. It's the only way I can squeeze out that last bit of the toothpaste.

On my way to work I saw my old schoolmate Shampoo O'Reilly. I said "Hi Timotei. Long-time no see." He said "Sorry I can't stop. That boy from Bangkok that was in our form at school has just offered me a good job." It just goes to show that the old school Thai still comes in handy now and again

So this toad said to the tadpole "Fancy a jar?" The tadpole said "Yes, ok. I wouldn't mind a little natter, Jack."

Two Amish fundraisers rang my doorbell at 2 a.m. this morning jingling their collection boxes. I said "Call back in the morning." They said "We can't. We're Mennonites."

I recently got lost at an exhibition of cinema art in a gallery under re-furbishment, but got back on track thanks to a small robot pointing the way to the ART TOUR DETOUR.

So Orville said to ventriloquist, Keith Harris "I wish I could fly way up to the sky, but I can't." Luckily, Wilbur Wright was the more motivated of the two brothers. [1]

So I told the owner of the grocery shop that when I opened the tin of milk that he'd sold me I found it was empty. He said "What do you expect? It says it's evaporated on the tin." He suggested I wait a day or two to see if it came back but I don't believe in Rein-Carnation.

My uncle went sailing up the Amazon where he was crushed by a giant Giaconda. It's the same as an Anaconda but has an enigmatic smile.

---

[1] Orville is a UK ventriloquist's dummy in the form of a giant baby bird.

I was forced to go to court the other day because I wouldn't disclose the secret ingredients of a rum based cocktail. In the end they served me with a subpoena colada.

My brother said to me the other day "Have you ever considered the infinity of space?" I said "To be honest, that's the furthest thing from my mind at the moment."

So then he asked me if I ever thought about the landlocked country between Rumania and the Ukraine. I said "It's an area I've Moldova from time to time."

He's actually just gone into hiding after wetting the bed in a hotel and then trying to conceal the evidence. All because someone told him that you can get 10 years for matricide.

He's a person I'd describe as 'a little bit different'. For a start, he can never finish any project he starts. He's currently on his tenth attempt at designing a games console. I suggested that he call it *Intendo*.

He's an insecure hypochondriac. Last week he insisted on going to the testicles department at the local hospital for a check-up even though he's never ever been the least bit ticklish.

I can understand where he gets his insecurity from. When he was 10, we all laughed at him on Xmas day when mother dressed him up as a Chinese emperor, The Mikado. Serves him right! He should never have asked for a *Meccano* Set when he had a head cold.

He's fanatical about not wasting food. He's even got a donor kebab card in case he drops dead on his way home from the pub.

DONER CARD

IN THE EVENT OF MY DEATH I WOULD LIKE SOMEONE TO EAT MY KEBAB

He was sacked from his first part time job, playing a ghost in pantomime. All because he wouldn't say boo to a goose.

After that he went on a course to learn the basics of musical comedy and on the strength of that he was appointed resident clown at the home of the London Philharmonic Orchestra where he played the buffoon.

Then he tried his hand at being an investment florist. He started in peony shares, then tried stocks and finished up specialising in the fuchsias' markets. His problem was that he went for dark colours, not realising that 'the fuchsias bright, the fuchsias orange'.

After that he got a job as the welcome coordinator at a Welsh hyper-market. Every time, opera singer, Bryn Terfel came in, my brother would point to the biscuit aisle and sing "Fig a Roll, Fig a Roll, Fig a Roll." He did the same job in The States at Wall-Mart and got sacked for telling a native American who came into the store "Custards, last stand on the right."

When it comes to holidays my brother is a traditionalist who likes nothing better than to spend his summer break helping the local vet neuter female dogs. He says you can't beat a bucket and spayed holiday.

Friends have been praising him for scoring 30 points on Mastermind last week on his individual subject, *The Chemistry of Lettuce*. I really don't know what all the fuss is about. It's not rocket science is it?

So I said to this Scotsman "Does anyone in your family ride?" He said "My sister Genghis Khan but my brother Gymkhana."

Since we've had a new 4 x 4 my wife has had quite a few accidents. We've started to call her 'RV wall-banger.'

I saw two coal tits and a woodpecker the other day. Now I come to think of it, it was a funny looking snowman.

My brother received an explosive cheese in the post last week. I said "How did you handle it?" He said "Caerphilly."

So this judge came into court wearing sunglasses, dressed in a T shirt and Bermuda shorts. Well it was only a summary hearing.

So Nero turned to the guard who had just arrived with Mel Gibson dressed as a 19th century mutineer and said "For fornication's sake, I told you to FETCH A CHRISTIAN."

So I went to the most impatient tailor in the country. He said "How about a nice pin stripe?" I said "I'd prefer a check." He said "Suit yourself."

At the audition for the church pantomime, I said "This chimney sweep got his brush stuck up the ..." The vicar said "Sorry, no smut."

Just then I heard a long whistle and a small mouse like creature fell out of the sky. I thought "Someone's dropped a clanger."

So the choirmaster asked me if I wore dentures. I said "No, but I can sing falsetto."

I have a penchant for dancing on pub tables wearing only my underpants. I've managed to keep it under wraps so far but I'd be mortified if anything ever came out.

My brother has turned down the role of Bottom in *A Midsummer Night's Dream*. He said he couldn't be arsed.

My wife is in the attic with St Paul at the moment. Well, she's been nagging me for months for a loft conversion.

I was sunbathing by the pool when my wife walked by covered in guacamole. I said "Nice dip darling?"

I went to a lecture on the Baltic last week. It really is an irritating little creature.

So I said to this chap "I need to fake a fall in the house so I can claim on my insurance." He said "Have you tried Trip Advisor?"

My wife has just asked a rail-track maintenance engineer to Christmas lunch. She says you can't beat a points-setter at the Christmas table.

.My wife and I got lost on a coastal path tour of Normandy, France. Turned out we were stuck between Deauville and the deep blue sea. She's half French, half Welsh and very popular in Italy. That's because she is garlic bread.

It's only just struck me...that boomerang I threw away two minutes ago.

I can't agree with those people who argue that acupuncture is a pointless exercise.

The rules committee at my local golf club are getting much stricter. Last week they found a dead sheep in a bunker on the first fairway and they insisted that the driver of the JCB did not touch the sand with his scooper before removing it in one swing.

On our way to the polling station my wife and I were stopped by a member of the British Anatomical Party. I said "What's your constituency?" He said "70% water plus bits of nitrogen, carbon, calcium and a few other things."

My wife didn't speak to me on the way home from the Swimming Club's annual prize giving because when I toasted the synchronised swimming team winners I said "Bottoms up!"

My brother never knows when to shut up. Only last week he went to see a performance of a famous Requiem and started the audience singing "Faure's a jolly good fellow."

My brother recently joined a formation ballroom dancing team so that he could claim attendance allowance.

Then he asked the team to concentrate on the 'Quick-step' so that he could claim at the higher rate.

My wife didn't mind when I couldn't accompany her to the annual Flatulence Society dance because she already had plenty of pardoners for the excuse ME's.

When I was a teenager my father changed our family surname by deed poll to Nitrous Oxo-ide. It made us the laughing stock of the community.

I told my local scout group that if they took my grandmother on the ghost train they should make sure she was happy, didn't have any unexpected shocks, and occasionally feed her the odd cheese snack. All the way round I could hear them singing "Grin Gran. Ghouly! Ghouly! Ghouly! Ghouly! Ghouly! Wotsit? Grin Gran. Ghoul! Grin Gran. Ghoul!"

DÉJÀ VUE

THE CINEMA CHAIN SHOWING FILMS THAT SOUND FAMILIAR BUT WHICH MAY HAVE LOST THE PLOT

Insomniac father and son meet prospective new mum on New Year's Eve at top of Yorkshire town's highest building.

SLEEPLESS IN SETTLE

Nosy neighbour spends one day short of 8 weeks spying on Chinese family next door through the front room curtains.

55 DAYS AT PEEKING

Physics teacher panics and sends message to all students as a reminder of seminar to discuss Scottish based scientist and his theories of thermodynamics. (But there's a nasty surprise waiting in the gymnasium)

WE NEED TO TALK ABOUT KELVIN

Two movies directed by Quentin Tarantino about a woman on a mission to do away with whoever overcharged her, twice, for making traditional Scottish dress.

KILT BILL I and II

Absent minded CIA contract killer, Jason, becomes a Jehovah's Witness but is recognised by an old enemy when delivering leaflets. After killing 428 agents in self-defence, he becomes chief chaplain of the CIA.

THE BOURNE AGAIN CHRISTIAN

In a starkly contrasting film to others in the series about the Volkswagen Beetle car with a mind of its own, our hero turns cannibal and eats his cousin as the Pope addresses the city of Rome and the World in general.

HERBIE ATE ORBI

Hopelessly edited ten minute World War II epic with an all-star cast tells the story of Operation Market Garden at Arnhem

ABRIDGED TOO FAR

Clint Eastwood revisits old territory to fall in love as he photographs kitchen domestic appliances in Iowa.

THE FRIDGES OF MADISON COUNTY

The evil count returns, dripping wet, standing on the dining room table between the sprouts and the cauliflower.

DRACULA HAS RISEN FROM THE GRAVY

Trapped on the top shelf of the biggest airing cupboard in the world, the fire that had started among the neatly folded drying accessories begins to spread upwards causing panic on the higher shelves.

THE TOWELLING INFERNO

Price war starts in the West Indies as pieces of eight varieties of crust enclosed savoury snacks, including Steak and Kidney and Meat and Potato, are sold by ships' crews at competitive prices.

PIE RATES OF THE CARIBBEAN

Revelations galore as NASA releases footage, shot on video by first Americans on the moon, showing wreckage of a Viking long-ship and the remains of the quartet who made up its crew. These archive shots are the only evidence of a story of the amazing feat achieved by those intrepid explorers.

THE FOUR NORSEMEN OF THE APOLLO CLIPS

A New York gang have to cross rivals' territory on their way home to Coney Island but are plagued with anxieties about crossing the road, keeping their shirts tucked in to stay warm, hoping it doesn't rain, and, above all, that they won't get told off when they arrive home. Walter Hill's masterpiece of anxiety unleashed.

THE WORRIERS

Schoolgirls go missing after eating sandwiches in the outback as a mysterious Dickensian character with aspirations of World domination appears out of thin air.

PICKWICK AT HANGING ROCK

Voody, Cosmonaut Yuri and Mr and Mrs Potato Head save Anna K from under the wheels of a train in Pick Tsar's classic scripted animation film.

TOLSTOY STORY

Quaint story about the residents of a small Scottish island who go store crazy as a ship carrying tins of cat food is shipwrecked on the shoreline.

WHISKERS GALORE

A Russian princess enters hospital for a simple nose job, then apparently goes roaming off and is never seen again.

ANAESTHESIA

The most mundane of attractions are exaggerated out of all proportion in this documentary by a florid speaking Egyptian windbag taking us on a tour of the capital city.

THE PURPLE PROSE OF CAIRO

How Othcar outwitted the eth eth and thaved many from the conthentrathun campth.

SCHINDLER'S LISP

In a follow up to his highly unsuccessful documentary on the Egyptian capital, our intrepid documentary maker takes us to meet aged varicose vein sufferers as they carry out their duties in the oldest profession known to man.

THE PURPLE PROS OF CAIRO

A tweed-skirted old maid overcharges a naive South American evacuee for two pieces of bread, thinly spread with preserve, giving him only 50 cents change from his $5 Bill.

4.50 FROM PADDINGTON

She's at it again, this time giving $6.90 change from a $10 Bill to an actress who is looking for a tailor who over charged her twice for traditional Scottish dress.

3.10 FROM UMA

In the last of the series, Miss Marble targets the ex-wife of Bruce Willis, so that she can retire in peace to a quiet English village, St Mary Mead, Mother of God where someone is murdered every Sunday.

FOR A FEW DOLLARS, MOORE

January 1963, and as the winter weather closes in, a secret band of men with extraordinary powers meet for the first time to predict the future and save the UK from chaos. The true story behind the 'Marvel'-lous six who sat on the Pools Panel.

X MEN

COMING TO A CINEMA NEAR YOU

Fasten your chinstraps. A bumpy night is on the cards with the premiere of *Penguin: A Rock Hoppera* being beamed live from the feeding station at Regents Park Zoo to cinema venues around the country. (All rights reserved) A few seats left with restricted views in the Arctic Circle

Written by the Antarctic Monkeys, it stars Arab rap star, Polar Abdul in the title role as the deaf, dumb and blind bird impressionist who sure plays a mean Pingu. Forced to waddle in the London marathon, he is tricked into being wrapped up in silver foil but is saved when no-one can remove the tear strip. All ends happily when he is adopted by Elton John who gives him a job as a butler.

As an ice breaker, Ranulph Fiennes all late comers, who are then made to incubate an egg for the duration of the winter thus making it the only show in town to have a continuous standing ovation.

Bi-polar bears roam the aisles with 'For Sale' signs attached and free buckets of fish are available to throw as Abdul, and Nicold Kidman stand atop a giant Bull Seal and our hero hums **'One** day I'll fly away.' as dwarf effigies of once famous chocolate bars sing 'We could be Heroes'. Other songs include 'I am a Walrus' by Seal and 'P…P…P…pick up a penguin' sung by Iced T

A spectacular finale features Abdul leading the largest ever dance troupe assembled for a musical, high kicking 'The March of the Penguins' off the stage. But look out for the short fat Penguin at the back with the umbrella, looking for his dinner, dinner, dinner.....

BREAKING NEWS

London

Queen to recognise work of plasterers with annual award given for surfaces rendered.

Boston

Scientists discover that word 'Ball' is the B, all and end all. When interviewed Bat said 'All these years we've been together and I didn't have a clue. He's so self-effacing I still can't believe it.

Leeds

Fish and chip shops all over the UK are suffering from a shortage of deep fried German Sausages. A spokesman, calling for a complete overhaul of the supply system, hinted that the Industry would need to get Wurst before it got batter.

Coventry

Striking workforce turns out in numbers to examine 'scab' in great detail. Asked for a comment on the situation a Company spokesman said, "If you picket, it won't get better."

Berlin

'Jerry Springer, The Opera' opens to poor reviews. Critics particularly scathing on wandering performance of the star spaniel and called for the original American lead to be flown in to try to regain a degree of control.

Ontario

A zoo that names all its animals after characters in opera had a visit from the security services last week who questioned the Elk, Aida, for over an hour.

Nottingham

Puss in Boots, Susan Boyle, ruled out of pantomime, as yellow matter seeps through lace holes in her Doc Martins.

Bologna

Attendants at nearby Leaning Tower crowd control centre sacked for not minding their Ps and Qs.

Detroit

Man missing for 15 years at local Ford factory found in trunk of old Poplar in corner of the car park.

Heidelberg

Hanseatic League papers found in loft of house indicate existence of table football competition in 1400. Rumours of a vocabulary club called the Pundesliga also abound.

Middle East

Man claiming to have been on flying carpet trip found to have been under the influence of Djinn.

Jerusalem

Archaeologists discover remains of picnic hamper used by Arab Leader at time of the second Crusade with inscription 'To keep Saladin.'

SPECIAL FEATURE

Washington: November 2005

A team of Navy Seals was today called into action as a siege in the main tent of the visiting Moscow State Circus went into its 3rd day. Balancing beach balls on their noses and clapping their flippers to attract the attention of the man with the bucket of fish they entertained the crowd who had become restless after watching the trapeze artists for 2 days. A spokesman for the hostages said, "However highly they are viewed in the circus, once you've seen one painting of a swing you've seen them all."

A SWAT team that had been called in earlier were forced to return home to study for forthcoming exams.

The audience is being held hostage by Lonely the Clown who has a grudge against the circus. In a statement issued on the first day of the siege, South African born, Dwight Van Driver, said through sobs "I can't get my car in the grudge because of where they've erected the Big Top."

A police spokesman agreed that it was difficult for Lonely to park his car because of the guy ropes, but he felt that the clown had overstepped the mark in his size 22 plastic shoes and that his mournful face was all part of an act. The manager of the circus, Bill Wordsworth said "On the first day I saw Dwight with a host of golden daffodils in his arms, I wondered about Lonely as a clown".

Later:

Animal rights protesters besiege the siege at the Moscow State Circus to complain about the navy paint spray that was used on the seals by the owners earlier today. A spokesman for the paint company said "All this talk of clogging up their pores is ridiculous. Any animal rights protester worth his salt would know that seals have flippers. Now if they had turned up last week when we sprayed the lions with black and white stripes to fool the zebras I could understand, because we could not remove the paint from their feet

for love nor money. Luckily, Zelda, the bearded lady, had a spare

bucket of her special nail varnish remover and that did the trick."

Later:

Siege at the Moscow State Circus ends as Dwight puts a gun to his head and a white flag pops out in surrender. As he is led away a grim Aldi executive mumbled that his company would not sponsor this form of entertainment in the future.

Much later:

The crowds have left the big top but something is wrong. Smiley George, who people in the organisation think is an outdated clown, has spotted mounds of earth appearing in the ring overnight. There is a mole in the circus and future tense will be affected if Smiley can't find Karla, the fortune teller, to correct any punctuation errors in his shortly to be published memoir of the gypsy outfitter who supplied hot savoury snacks to previous employees of the organisation, entitled (Pause for breath) 'Tinker Tailor Sold Us Pies.'

WHO AM I?

An after dinner game f\or all the family.

Guess my identity in the least number of clues to win the game. Write down your guess when you think you know the answer and mark it with the clue number. Only 1 guess is allowed and you will need to wait until all answers are in before the solution may be revealed.

Clue 1

I am the eponymous anti-hero of a book and a film.

Clue 2

I was born and raised on an island where conflict amongst families was rife.

Clue 3

Eventually I was forced to leave for America, though I could neither write nor speak English.

Clue 4

I was generally known by a title bestowed upon me by others, yet never spoke to them about my past.

Clue 5

I changed a great deal over the course of the three films which bear my name, becoming more sophisticated with the passing of time, gaining iconic status within 'the genre.'

Clue 6

Once I had built a reputation in America, many people came to see me but most feared, rather than liked, me.

Clue 7

In my first film I was small in stature but had a huge screen presence, making it big on Broadway during the 1930s.

Clue 8

I had eyes for only one girl in my life, but, coming from different sides of the tracks, our future together was doomed from the start, although, at times, I held her future in the palm of my hand.

Clue 9

I still couldn't speak English at the end of the films, but if I had been able, I may have said 'Look Ma, top of the world.'

Clue 10

Constantly at odds with the authorities I eventually went on the run and died, unarmed, in a hail of bullets, though my epitaph was that it was 'beauty killed the beast.'

ANSWER AFTER NEXT SECTION

COMING TO A TELEVISION NEAR YOU

WHEN THE OIL RAN OUT IN DALLAS THE FEUDING
FAMILIES MOVED TO THE WELSH VALLEYS, WHERE
THE ONLY DERRICKS WERE THE NAMES OF THE
LOCALS' PET SHEEP

BUT WHICH FAMILY WOULD CONTROL THE VALLEYS?

IT'S THE EWE-INGS V THE BAA-RNS ALL OVER AGAIN

DOWLAIS

A TRITE AND CLICHÉD PRODUCTION

OF AN A465 ROAD MOVIE WITH VICTORIAN

PRINCIPLES

DIRECTED BY SHORN PEN

STARRING

SHEER HER NIGHTLY AS FLU-ELLEN

BAA-BAA BELL GEDDES AS MISS SMELLY

AND FEATURING

SHORN 'CAN' HAIRY

AS A

JOCK QUEUING FOR HIS PENSION AT THE POST OFFICE

WITH

PAT AND RICK DUFFY AS 2 LOCAL BOBBIES

WHO CHANGE AFTER A SHOWER

FLEECITY KENDAL AS PAM BAA-RNS

CHARLIE STILTON AS THE POISONED DWARF

WITH GUEST APPEARANCES BY LARRY HOGMAN AS THE PIG FARMER

AND

DOLLY THE SHEEP FROM COLOGNE, WITH HER GERMAN SHEPHERD,

HERMANN, GRRRING AT THE CAST THROUGHOUT THE FILM.

CAMEO APPEARANCES BY RUSTLE BRAND AND MERINO HARA

CRIMINAL SCREENPLAY DEVISED BY AUTHORESS BAA-BAA OVINE

MUSIC BY THE RAM MOANS

MISS NIGHTLY'S JEWELLERY SUPPLIED BY RAM BLING OF RAMSGATE

DISTRIBUTED IN THE MIDDLE EAST BY RAMMER 'DAN'

THE PRODUCERS WISH TO STATE THAT NO SHEEP

WERE BAA-BAA CUED DURING THE FILMING OF THIS MOVIE

WHO AM I?

KING KONG

A SCOTTY POTTY DICTIONARY

English words and phrases uttered 'north of the border' in Scotland have a totally different meaning to that which one would find in a standard dictionary. Here are some brief examples not listed in alphabetical order but in relation to frequency of use. An ability to think in a 'mock' Scottish accent will help the reader to better understand the 'translation' which, in many cases, reflects the possessiveness and negativity inherent in the Scottish 'psycho.'

Hogmanay

Piggy bank savings.

Matrimony

Savings I put away towards a haircut.

Mascara

My Swiss Army penknife.

Marriage Guidance Counsellor

My rock climbing instructor.

Mahogany

My pet pig Annie that I originally thought was female.

Mappa Mundi

My list of the pubs that my father frequents at the beginning of the week.

Madonna

My kebab.

Madonna kebabs

My pet donkey, Barbara

Barbara

Mascarpone

My mother is to take the part of a notorious Chicago gangster.

(Local Amateur Dramatics)

Malaga

My 6 cans of Special Brew.

Och Aye

Line technology used in the Scottish Tennis Championships.

Och Aye the Noo

A more up to date version of Och Aye.

Ouija board

Public house price list for wines and spirits.

Mafeking

A famous siege that lasted 217 days.

Nomad

I'm relatively sane.

Nomadic

I'm definitely not the father.

Nepal

I'm a bit of a loner.

Nepalese

I'd prefer not to involve the local constabulary.

Neighbours

The only pigs I have left are sows.

Cacophony

Do you use these toilets on a regular basis?

Maharajah

Hogmanay substitute for big nights out.

Mahout

Sound I make if I need to draw somebody's attention.

Hootenanny

Like my Gran for instance.

Nemesis

I'm a confirmed bachelor.

Non Compos mentis

I'm sold out of spearmint flavoured manure.

Negro

I'm a dwarf.

Mason-Dixon Line

My son, Richard, is currently connected to the internet.

Nescafe

There is obviously some reason why your neck is unprotected against
the cold.

Newark, New Jersey

When my mother heard that I'd lost the use of my legs she bought
me a pullover to cheer me up.

DICTIONARY CORNER

The relevance and continued existence of certain words in the English dictionary is not only under threat from advances in technology but also from articles such as this which seek to make a mockery of the meanings of long established dictionary entries. Here are a few for which it may already be too late.

Aficionado

Sign found on the entrance to a house of a 'born again' Christian.

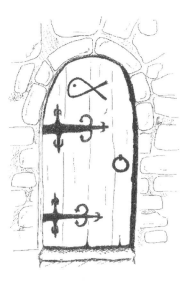

Allergy

An aversion to Sacha Baron Cohen.

Apparatchik

A talking bird that can recite the Communist Manifesto from infancy.

Apennines

A range of hills in Yorkshire, 'Ay Up.'

Arsenic

A possible danger one may encounter when shaving the backs of one's legs.

Barbiturates

Crisps, olives and nuts.

Beautician

A really good painting by an Italian Renaissance artist.

Bow-wow

Deluxe archery set that daddy wouldn't buy me for Christmas

Buffalo

A warm welcome at the nudist camp.

De-carbonate

What one lifts to reveal the car's engine.

Eugenics

Underwear for the slightly larger lady.

Fulcrum

A duck who can't eat another thing.

Hootenanny (Note difference to Scotland)

The olfactory organ of a female goat.

Molest

Descriptive of the most velvety skinned, tiny eyed and eared, reduced hind limbed but powerfully front quartered, large pawed creature that will ever dig up your back lawn overnight.

Moussaka

A small but dear Greek pie.

Oddity

A poem missing the second, fourth, sixth and eighth lines.

Pharisees

Jewish binoculars.

Posthumous

Chickpea dip available by mail order.

Pudenda

Time to serve the cheese and biscuits.

Supercilious

Having a clown's face painted on one's backside.

IDIOMS

Bucket List

A tendency to walk lopsidedly due to having one's foot stuck in a pail.

Bump start

Puberty.

Cement one's relationship

Bury the wife under the patio

Cross Dresser

Person with an ugly temper first thing in the morning.

Halcyon Days

State of shock induced by having been hit on the head with a Kingfisher.

Harem Scarum

Eunuch wearing a 'Scream' mask.

J

Papal Bull

Holy Father scores 50 with a single dart.

Privileged position

Balanced on the rim of the toilet bowl.

Tickety Boo

Popular pastime of old-style bus conductors who would conceal

themselves until unpaid passengers were about to alight from the bus.

It is understood that Fare Dinkum is an Australian version of the

same pastime

Tickled pin

To have made Alicia Beth Moore giggle and scream by placing your
fingers between her ribs[2]

---

[2] Alicia Beth Moore is an American singer songwriter and actress known as
'Pink.'

CHANTS HEARD DURING THE FINAL STAGES

OF GLOBAL COMPETITIONS

Supporters: 1964 Insects' Football World Cup Final

"Earwigo, Earwigo, Earwigo."

Competitors during the changing of ends at the 1968

Hermaphrodites of the Year Championship

"Sing when you're women. You only sing when you're women."

Liverpool team about to be eliminated at the 1926 'Spell the

name of A.A. Milne's Donkey' competition

"E I add E O we're gonna win the cup."

Supporters: 1951/52 World Individual Sculpting Championships

"You're not singing, Henry Moore."

Competitors: WMD sponsored final for the 2008 'Blair/Bush Impersonators of the Year' Trophy

"And now you're gonna believe us, and now you're gonna believe us."

Someone in the gallery after every shot hit by every competitor in every USA Undertaker's Golf Championship since 1888

"In the hole."

Opponents at 1999 German Wheelchair Basketball final

"You'll never walk, Cologne."

Parrots' complaining of judge's vested interest at the 1952 Final of the World's Heaviest Flying Bird Competition

"The referee's a bustard."

Appreciation for the winner of Caledonian Nancy Boy of the Year 2010

"Oh Flower of Scotland."

Loutish song sung by 2013 Glyndebourne audience at the end of outdoor operatic concert with free drinks

"And we were sinking 'Pimms' with arias."

DR KINLAY'S FACEBOOK

"Why is it that the pills you self-prescribed have given you buck teeth, floppy ears, and a craving for carrots?"

Dr K: "I've discovered that I have mixed up my doses."

"I am consistently saying 'sit, deafer a tension.' Why?"

Dr K: "You have 'a tension deafer sit' disorder."

"Members of my church choir are experiencing dizzy spells during morning service. What could be the cause?"

Dr K: "Your chorister stall may be too high."

Why do I get angry when I hear people say 'a' 'e' 'I' and 'o'?

Dr K: "You have irritable vowel syndrome."

"How much longer will I need to wait for specialist treatment for my herpes zoster and haemorrhoids?"

Dr K: **"You are currently third in the shingles and fifth in the all bum charts.**

"My next door neighbour, Mr Wladislav Zerwinski, thinks he's turning into a frog. Is this possible?

Dr K: **"Well he does sound a tad polish"**

"I appear to be developing a fear of train spotters. Is this common?"

Dr K: **"Yes. You are suffering from Anorak-sia Nervosa."**

"Why do my eyes itch at the opticians when I read words like 'and', 'plus' and 'with'? "

Dr K: **"It's symptomatic of a conjunctive eye test."**

"My husband gets very irritable when asked to total up any figures. Is there any treatment available?"

Dr K: "Yes. Adenoids are easily treatable these days."

"I think I'm an Italian cow with deja vu"

Dr K: "Yes. I think you've been a herbivore too."

"I've just returned from a photo shoot in the Antarctic and fear I've developed piles from sitting on the ice. What should I do?"

Dr K: "Please call me again once your Polaroids have fully developed."

"I've had a sudden urge to take all the chairs out of the administration and accounts departments of my company. Can you explain?"

Dr K: "You are becoming a little too stand-offish."

"I've been told a lobotomy will cure my sagging backside. Is this true?"

Dr K: "It will not do anything for the condition but it will make you care less about the way you look."

BREAKING NEWS

London

Prize for 'Dual Purpose Object of the Year' won by woman who invented female contraceptive device with in-built stimulator. Judges commented "Even second place would have been a real feather in her cap."

London

ITV is to screen a new comedy version of Mildred Pierce set in 1763. A spokesperson said "We just wanted it to have that Georgian Mildred feel."[3]

Nepal

Climbers descending Mount Everest today confirmed that they had passed the crew of HMS Bounty who were on the way up. One climber said "We thought they were ever so rude, passing us without saying a word, until we realised they were mutineers."

---

[3] 'George and Mildred was a popular 1970s UK sit-com

Glasgow

Entertainment world shocked as The Krankies join with remnants of a 1960s pop band to tour as 'Fan, Dabby, Dozy, Beaky, Mick and Tich.' [4]

Belfast

After clashes with political protesters last year, Irish ornithologists have announced that future Bill Oddie Sunday marches will be moved to a Thursday.[5]

Dublin

The funeral of Ireland's oldest bog-man and fuel cutter took place today. In line with his wishes he was buried in his back garden with a headstone inscribed 'Here lies Fergal Muldoon. May he rest in Peat.'

Dublin

---

[4] The Krankies are the pride of Scottish culture, a hysterically funny male/female duo whose catchphrase is 'Fan Dabby Dozy.'. The pop band referenced was Dave Dee, Dozy, Beaky, Mick and Tich.

[5] Bill Oddie, a former member of the popular comedy trio 'The Goodies' is now best known as a charismatic, BBC television ornithologist.

Irish amateur world piggyback champion Willy O'Reilly announces he is turning pro because he wants something more out of the sport than just a pat on the back.

Greenland

Eskimos join Brits worried about changing patterns in the language of their young as latest reports confirm almost 8 out of 10 children now end every sentence with word 'Inuit?'

Madrid

Jewish bullfighter now clear favourite to top Spanish Xmas pop chart with rock version of 'The Ole and The Oy Vey.'

Hollywood

Female stars, Kate Winceyette and Kiera Nightie set to battle it out for lead role in new version of 'The Pyjama Game.'

Cardiff

Rumanian rugby team take umbrage at singing of the Welsh National anthem prior to the start of play. Match begins 5 minutes late after they accept that crowd were singing 'Gwlad, Gwlad' and not eulogising the source of the Count Dracula legend.[6]

London

Tabloid newspaper is reprimanded by press regulators for publishing details of the rapid escape of a female Q.C, following a serious assault. Headline: 'Rogered Barrister runs 4 minute mile in Oxford' considered inappropriate.

Canterbury

Vicar blames new font for mistake made at christening. The mother of Times New Roman Rhodes was last night too upset to comment.

Jackson, Mississippi

---

[6] Gwlad is Welsh word for 'Country'

Farmer devastated as dove cote and chicken coop burnt to the ground. Police suspect re-emergence of the Coo Clucks Clan.

Oklahoma City

Police call off search for missing sewage farm worker after discovery of slurry with a fringe on top.

Salzburg

Two year old piano playing prodigy banned from music store for tinkling on the ivories

NEW RELIGIONS OF THE DAY

Hide and Sikhism

An offshoot of the religion founded in the fifteenth century by Guru Nanak, it was devised by members who wish to remain incognito. They firmly believe in resurrection and a day of retribution. Its mantra is 'Second Coming, Ready or Not.'

Budda'ism,

Originally confined to people living in the North East of England, but now reputedly spreading in all directions, it is the veneration of the Danish entity, Lerpak, and his Egyptian mystic, Anka, who wage a constant war with the false profit, Marge. Followers tend to be a little on the large side.

Balsamic Fundamentalism

Followers pour over the works of the God, Vinega, usurper of the throne long held by Heinz, the German God of Has-Beans with 57 personifications. Devotees are 'tossers', social climbers and mixers, the Toms and Olives of society. Followers traditionally dress in greens, know their onions and frequently exchange lettuce on the subject.

Hurry Krishna

Now acknowledged as the fastest religion in the world, its groups are a haven for alopecia sufferers and are frequently seen in city centres dressed in bed linen sponsored by Orange. Rumours that they are to have their own 100m sprint title at the next Olympics have been described as balderdash.

Zorro Austrianism

Religious sect, allegedly founded by Arnold Schwarzenegger, follows the teachings of Don Diego De Le Vegan, a mystery man or woman who, dressed in black hat, mask and cape, took revenge against meat eaters in cheap American 'B' movies.

Arnold reputedly had a spiritual moment in a restaurant where, when suffering with a head cold, he saw two dishes listed which he read as a portent of doom;

Chilly Conk, Arnie? –Vegetable-Bury Arnie.

The American arm of the sect is allegedly led by Catherine Zeta Jones, who apparently signs all correspondence with just the single letter Z

LATEST BOOK REVIEWS

ANTON CHEKHOV

Cheeky co-presenter of 'I'm a Celebrity. Get me out of here' tries his hand at literary criticism in a poorly punctuated book.

À LA RECHERCHE DU TEMPS PERDU

Marcel Proust does a Nostradamus in this 1913 futuristic view of what would happen if Newcastle United F.C. were ever to be managed by a man called 'Perdu' or similar.

THE TWO RONNIES' JOKE BOOK

A criminal joke book by Messrs Biggs and Kray that could make the ideal stocking filler at Xmas, bearing in mind that after the festive season one could put the stocking over one's head and go out to hold up a Post Office.

UNDER MILK, WOOD

Dylan Thomas' unfinished first attempt at compiling an English/Welsh dictionary.

THE BATMAN POEMS OF DYLAN THOMAS

Another incomplete work notable only for the depiction of Robin's heartfelt anguish at Batman's growing obesity in the poignant 'Donut, go gently into that Dark Knight.'

THE PRIVATE LETTERS OF IKE AND TINA TURNER

Family of General and ex-President Eisenhower still to comment on revelations from the man who wrote 'The Hitler Diaries' for 'The Sunday Times.'

GENITALIA

Subtitled 'The hidden gems of Italy' this guide book catalysed the eventual departure of the Publishing Company's CEO in 2013.

GARDENERS QUESTION TIME WITH STEPHEN HAWKING

The concept of 'Time' is discussed in this, the first of a series of books of interviews by prominent horticulturalists. Next up is 'Gardeners Question Cookery with Michel Roux.'

ANDRE AMPERE'S GUIDE TO PICNIC BASKETS AND PICNICKERS

This electrifying story of how Ampere came to invent the picnic basket is currently on sale at all branches of 'The Works' under ohm improvements. We wish we could give it a plug but our advice is to resist watt is an enlightening but shockingly awful read.

ANDRE AMPERE'S GUIDE TO PINK KNICKERS

While researching his book on picnickers, Ampere inadvertently Gogoled[7] 'pink knickers' (at least that's his story) and from that time forth became infatuated with them. The book is a pale imitation of The Bumper Book of Freudian Slips and deserves to be relegated to the bottom drawers of the bedroom units where it belongs.

AUGUST STRING BAG'S 'TAKING TOWELS TO THE BEACH'

Taking towels to the beach will never seem the same again after reading this gripping Swedish saga of one family's summer spent coming to terms with German tourists on the sun beds at their local beach.

---

[7] Gogol was a Russian browser of the day frequently used by spiritualists seeking to contact the souls of the recently departed.

POTPOURRI AND BENT CUTLERY

Uri Geller tells the world what he would do if he became Holy Father

and how many canteens of cutlery he ruined with his fork and spoon

bending act.

BREAKING NEWS

LONDON

Prestigious new Barby-Ken Arts Centre opened by Dolly Part-on, the world's first self-assembly doll. Manufacturing Company, Dolly Mixtures have been in the Doldrums for some years but believe Dolly will be their salvation. Brass band plays 'Hello Dolly' as the doll self assembles in front of large crowd who gasp when singer with the band gets to line, "You're looking swell, Dolly" Who said inflation was under control?

OXFORD

Artistic 'Fight of the Century' takes place between Ford 'Mad Ox' Ford and Ford 'Mad Ox' Brown, leading hard cases for rival gangs operating the salons of the rich and famous. Onlooker describes their behaviour as 'oxymoronic'.

LONDON

Prototype for original Dolly Part-on revealed together with Dolby Sound earphones which are on sale from 9 till 5

LONDON

Gilbert and Sullivan Society battle it out with American millionaire for original artwork for the advertising leaflet prepared for 'The Gondoliers'. Obvious breakdown in communication at the time now makes the item in question one of the most sought after pieces of theatre memorabilia in existence.

London

Barby-Ken exhibition of Dolly Part-on closes with Simon Rattle leading The Last Night of The Prams featuring songs from Buggy Malone and Carousel. The event is jointly sponsored by Smothercare and Pampas of Argentina.

Newcastle

Damien Hurst's 'Magnum Opus' goes on show. Animal cruelty organisations query how he managed to stuff a cat through the neck of a champagne bottle.

London

Royal princess fails to harness her anger at publication in Hoarse and Hounded of her original bridle photographs. Stable hands say she really has bit between her teeth.

Jerusalem

Scientists reveal fool proof test for Jewish ultra-orthodoxy is as simple as placing a small piece of litmus paper on the tongue. If it turns red you're Hasidic.

Coventry

Planners meeting to discuss ways and means of revitalising Britain's soulless 'concrete jungle' city centre areas suggest going back to square one and starting again. Luftwaffe to be contacted re possible implementation dates.

London

Newly discovered Agatha Christie play about 5 men trapped in a lift receives poor reviews as only one left alive for last act. Critics said it was a foregone conclusion.

Caracas

Venezuelan authorities refute suggestion that the country was discovered by a gondolier who had gone fishing and been swept out to sea. The Venice Whalers Society insist that the claim has some merit.

Miami

Organiser of 'Best Sun Tan of the Year Contest 'criticised by other competitors after walking away with the title himself. Local paper reported him as having put the rest of the entrants in the shade.

Adelaide

Australian marsupial impressionist and cross dresser Danny La Roo to play the lead in plaintive tale of the short life of a baby kangaroo who ends up in a tin of dog food. 'Pal Joey' is expected to go on tour in the New Year.

Tokyo

Mass suicide of partially deaf ex-army veterans reported at end of New Zealand diva operatic concert when member of audience shouted 'Hurrah Kiri' in appreciation of fine performance.

Moscow

Comrade Stalin sacks head of Broadcasting because pogroms were running later day after day. Stalin thanks deputy head of Broadcasting for bringing dyslexia induced error to his attention.

Moscow

Vacancies announced for new head and deputy head of Pogroming at Broadcasting House. Old heads displayed on spikes outside main entrance. Pravda forecasts 'Hedonistic Days Ahead.'

Paris

New fashion show opens of clothes cut from famous newspapers of the world modelled by Heads of State in Fancy Dress. David Cameron arrives as body builder wearing an FT costume but show is stolen by Vladimir Putin who makes headline in *Figaro* next day 'The Devil Wore Pravda'

Sheffield

Dwarf cattle farmer who stands on box to take all his shots wins World Snooker Championship but causes controversy when he unfolds his long branding iron with mark of the cross as aid to reaching long shots. As they say 'The rest is history.'

Minnesota

Mayo clinic discovers new filling for tuna sandwich.

Hollywood

Dwarf analogue lady included in digital version of 'Twin Peaks'

L. P.'s GUIDES

Following the success of his book 'The Gobby Twin', L.P. Artly acted as a go-between for the OPU from the late 1950s to the late 1980s, visiting country after country, assessing cities, peoples and cultures, and recording his findings for posterity.

Fondly known by his fan base as L.P. he was considered 'groovy' in the 1960s and 1970s during which time he sadly developed a craving for 'the needle' that was to keep him going for all of his working life. He suffered from shingles collections in his later years and more use of bad needles caused constant scratching, making him jumpy to the extent that he lost the quality of recording that had made him a success in his early years.

During his career, he had, under various global covers, taken part in 33 and one third revolutions, his demise coming only when his cover was blown in the early stages of the digital revolution, led ironically by his protégé, C.D.

He vinylly took early retirement at the end of the 1980s and for many years frequented charity shops and car boot sales, trying to attract passers-by but becoming more and more warped as he grew older.

After almost thirty years in the wilderness, he has now been 'rediscovered', and has begun a series of up to date travel guides for the inexperienced traveller.

L. P's GUIDE TO FRANCE

'France is a foreign country. They do things differently there.'

The first mention of the French may be found in the 410 BC research paper, 'The Frogs', by the Greek anthropologist, Aristophanes.

Their favourite word is' NON' which they use extensively during political negotiation.

They think themselves cultured yet cannot come to terms with the concept of The Teletubbies, constantly repeating the question 'Who Laa-Laa?'

Their favourite place is the countryside where they like to sit on fences.

TRAVEL TIPS

If planning to visit by air, avoid airlines with PAN in their name as they almost never-never land.

Paris' main airport is manufactured almost entirely from a form of stone named after a former president. De Gaulle stone, like the man whose name it bears, is very hard to remove and can be a constant source of pain.

BRONZE STATUE SITUATED OUTSIDE ARRIVALS

The airport is famed for its large sloping conk-course, where the sound of ol' factory organs is constant.

If planning to leave by ferry, use Dunkirk only in times of emergency as delays are unavoidable, queues tend to be long and the standard of vessel can vary enormously.

English visitors tend to favour the Stunner Line because of the built in stair lift system between decks which allows paralytic drunks quicker and safer access to the car decks from the bars below. Obesity is also well catered for by the Roll on Roll off system employed for the overweight foot passenger.

Party goers may use the Brian Ferry 'Rock Sea Music' line which operates between Plymouth and Rocks Off whenever the French crew are not on strike.

If air or sea is not to your liking, you have the option of the train service which runs from London to the stock cube yards of the Guard de Knorr in Paris. This service is operated by a Company whose motto is 'Oui'll take you anywhere for all your Euros, Ta.' This service used to run from Waterloo but after constant moans from the French it was moved to St Pancreas which resulted in the end o'crying on their part.

ROAD TIPS

If you have to drive in France remember;

A bien tot is not a French vehicle recovery service.

You will never see a sign that reads 'France welcomes careful drivers.'

The Paris Périphérique ring road is actually a Formula 3 race track.

French cars are normally Citroens driven by lemons, although their favourites are the Morris Chevalier and its smaller version, Morris Minor.

THINGS TO DO AND SEE

Take boat trips on the Garonne, named after the friendly embarkation instruction of the boat owners.

See Rouen, home to the French 'Bean', Rouen Atkinson and smell the chard (remains of Joan of Arc).

Visit the newly opened Bayeux Tapas tree, to eat freshly picked Spanish snacks before taking a look at a long piece of embroidery.

See the Louvre- Doors Exhibition before visiting the grave of Jim Morrison, inventor of the entrée. Then stroll around the famous Paris cemetery, while the kids play the old French card game, Pair La Chairs.

Go horse racing and read 'N'aies pas Peur', the French equivalent of The Racing Post.

Try poaching without fear of prosecution on 'Bass Steal' day.

Visit The Pompey Do Centre to see the massive collection of dog excrement found on the streets of Portsmouth.

Take in the exhibition of voice controlled home entry systems at The Quai D'Orsay.

And last but not least: should you happen to be in France on the 29th February, join the nation in their quadrennial performance of Le Leap Frog, where people of all ages come out of their houses, offices, shops and factories at daybreak to act out the age old ritual celebrating their emergence onto dry land which began the process of the ascent of Man. Germans have a similar ritual where husbands jump over the backs of their wives before opening a bottle of Leap Frau Milk for breakfast.

COMING SHORTLY

CLASSIC TELEVISION

PRESENTS

ROLLED AL'S

'TAILS OF THE UNEXPECTED'

THE OPU POETRY PRIZE (2014)

This year's entry was particularly strong in both the original and adapted classifications and those ditties to make the read offs are listed below.

First Prize:

ENTENTE CORDIAL AT THE OPU

Henri Swaki, Mali ponse,

Flew in from zee South of France

To attend his Alma Mater

For the Order of the Garter

Christmas meeting with the Queen

Who'd been joined by the French 'Bean'

Monsieur Atkinson was Rouen's

Master of the subtle nuance

There to ask the OPU

Through our man from Timbuktu,

Was there any outside chance

We'd allow a man from France

Into our esteem-ed ranks

The first student of the Francs.

There to study punned aerobics,

We said "NON! WE'RE XENOPHOBICS.

Reapply at some time nigh

You never know, 'cochons' may fly."

Second Prize:

ODE TO THE TAXMAN

Year ending April, 2012: £22,458.37p

Third Prize:

PLAYING WITH WORDS

Now and then meet this and that

To practice their word playing

This and now and then all stay

But that goes without saying.

IN THE STYLE OF EDMUND CLERIHEW BENTLEY

Edmund Clerihew,

Whose real name was Mary- Lou

Took tea without the lemon in

To prove she wasn't feminine.

––––––––––

Barack Obama

Invented Cinerama

To get a bigger picture

Of Superman by Nietzsche.

––––––––––

Mohandas Karamchand Ghandi

Could knock Raj ladies bandy

By showing them his passive

Disobedience was massive.

Bill and Ben

The flowerpot men

Have done a dirty deed

They've baked the tortoise in its shell

After smoking little weed

———————————

The stately Holmes of England

Was a wonderful detective

But his partner, Doctor Watson

Was a little bit defective

His elder brother Mycroft

Was also quite a smarty

But none of them was half as bright

As evil Moriarty.

AN ODE TO AN AGEING TELETUBBY'S URINARY

TRACT WRITTEN BY A SHEEP

Old bloodied old bladder,

Life goes on. Baa

Laa-laa! How the life goes on.

Old bloodied old bladder,

Life goes on. Baa

Laa-laa! How the life goes on.

And if you want some fun,

Take "Old bloodied bladder"

(May also be sung to a popular tune of The Beatles)

VARIATIONS ON A THEME OF THOMAS GRAY

The curfew tolls the knell of parting day

The ploughman nimbly vaults the bales of hay

And jumps o'er graveyard tombstones where they lay

And flick flacks over mourners as they pray

Agility in a Country Churchyard

The next eve as he vaults o'er those that pray

The ploughman coughs and brings up something grey

So calls in at the chemist on the way

To buy a can of cut price nasal spray

Allergy in a Country Churchyard

For the sake of propriety it was decided to omit

Allegedly in a Country Churchyard

THE ADDAMS FAMILY VISIT THE OLD

VICARAGE, GRANCHESTER

'Stands the church clock at ten to three

And is there honey still for tea?'

Said Pugsley to his uncle, Fester

Outside the Vicarage, Granchester

'For if there is I feel that we

Could go there as a family.

Wednesday, Morticia, Gomez too

Not cousin It, she's got the 'flu

TAILS OF THE UNEXPECTED

QUIZ TIME WITH THE OVAHEADS

(FILMS ARE NOT THEIR SPECIALITY)

Q: Which film portrayed the indignities faced by a disabled US soldier returning home after Vietnam?

A: It Shouldn't Happen to a Vet

Q: Name any film to vividly portray Christ's suffering and crucifixion.

A: The Long Good Friday

Q: Which film told the story of 'Britain's Got Talent' winner, opera star, Paul Potts?

A: The Killing Fields

Q: Who composed the music for 'Nightmare on Elm Street'?

A: Freddie and the Dreamers

Q: What was the subtitle of Terminator II?

A: Vera Drake

Q: Which film told the story of one man's fight to save refugees in the Rwandan civil war?

A: Tootsie

Q: Complete the title, E.T., The...

A: French Connection

Q: Name the film in which a famous Scottish born actor plays detective, searching for a killer of monks in a medieval monastery.

A: Greyfriars Bobby

Q: Name any Clint Eastwood film with scenes supposedly shot in the UK.

A: The Outlaw Joe Sees Wales

.

Q: Name any film to feature a cricket match?

A: Angela's Ashes

GENERAL KNOWLEDGE QUIZ

Well now you know what to expect try this general knowledge quiz.

1: Which film comedy actor of the 1930s invented the camping toilet?

2: Which niche musical composer and singer of the early twentieth century invented the more generally used portable toilet?

3: Which Shakespearean character says "Well indeed to goodness, there's lovely isn't it? Saucepan bach? "

4: It used to be 'Tulips from Amsterdam' but which song is now the most sung about that city in question?

5: Which star of the silver screen had a life saving device at sea named in their honour?

6: Who would be the perfect actress to play the invisible woman?

7: Which castrated rooster was Batman's constant companion?

8: Which Israeli politician is really an undercover internet browser?

9: Which of Peter Sellers' films features a bird in the title?

10: The giant condor of the Andes has an automatically adjustable wing span. When he takes his wife to work in the morning he flies west with a 100 % span but when he goes to pick her up in the evening it reduces to 50%. Why?

Answers to follow...

ART DECO

NEWS FROM THE WORLD OFART

The OPU Gallery is to stage 3 new photographic exhibitions

A retrospective of Page 3 archive shots entitled

'All The Nudes Still Fit for Print.'

A collection of Scandinavian photographs of cooked egg dishes called 'Omelette Prints of Denmark'

A ground-breaking, secretly shot montage of lightly dusted folders marked 'Top Secret-No Evidence of Weapons of Mass Destruction in Iraq' exhibited under the title of 'Fresh Prints of Blair.'

Articles in this month's 'Gallery' magazine include:

Pointillism: Is it just old Pollocks?

Will a Sekonda be found to support the motion to cancel the exhibition of Rembrandt's luminous masterpiece 'The Night Watch?'

Was Grandma Moses the 'Banksy' of ancient Egypt? 'Let My People Go' hieroglyphics found sprayed in the most inaccessible of places on pyramids in the Valley of the Kings

Eyebrows are raised as UK Benefits Agency unveils William Yeames' painting 'And when did you last see your father?' as the focal point of a new office block reception area. The trainee manager of the Agency who once attended Art College said "Dadaism is our new keyword."

A vintage Space Hopper recently sold in New York for £5,000,000 is to go on show with a newly discovered Toulouse le Trekkie painting of the 'Star-ship Enterprise'. 'Breakfast at the Klingon Cafe' is painted in the same style as Edward Hopper's other works depicting American life (1930-1950) but appears to have more bounce.

Norwegian Arts Council unveils huge statue of the painter of 'The Scream'. Monster Munch has been particularly popular with children.[8]

Vincent van Gogh's 'The Potato Eaters 'is to take pride of place at the 'Tate À Tate' exhibition that opens at the prestigious gallery next year. Sponsored by Spud U Lick, it is forecast to be the smash hit of the new season's crop of pot boilers in the art world and will be opened by selected members of the cast of the cult film 'M*A*S*H' .and a man from Clydach in South Wales who is hoping to find a baked potato

---

[8] Monster Munch was a popular baked corn snack in the UK

ANSWERS TO THE GENERAL KNOWLEDGE QUIZ

1: W C Fields

2: W C Handy...'the father of the 'B'loos'

3: False Taff

4: 'How much is that doggy in the window?'

5: George Raft

6: Faye Dunn Away

7: Well, have you ever seen Batman without his **Capon?**

8: Benjamin net 'n Yahoo

9: Only Toucan Play

10: The sun is in his eyes!

BREAKING NEWS

CARDIFF

Classic fairy tale given new slant with release of allegorical Welsh animation film set in a small town in the Welsh valleys.

BAMPI

Seen through the eyes of a loving grand-daughter, who imagines all the characters as animals from her storybook, BAMPI tells the story of her grandfather who as a young boy was left homeless when his mother was shot and killed by a lone gunman while out walking in the forest.

Abandoned by his father who goes mad with grief, Bampi is adopted by Thumper, a disco bouncer and Flower, a gay drugs pusher, who teach him the rules of survival in a world where danger lurks behind every tree and bush.

Bampi suffers the trials and tribulations of forest life in a coming of age movie with a difference and in a climactic final quarter, finds redemption in the shape of a doe, a deer, a female deer, ray, a drop of golden (sorry wrong film) named Faline who he rescues from the clutches of a pack of wild dogs.

In a formulaic ending, Bampi and Faline are married and have twins, one of which is the father of the narrator, Bampi locates his father and manages to find a place for him in a council run care home, Thumper renounces violence and turns to the Church and Flower settles down with a long term partner, all living happily ever after, just as they would in real life.

AN ABSURD LOOK AT THE LIVES OF FAMOUS PEOPLE FROM FRENCH HISTORY

JOAN OF ARC

During a heat-wave in the Fourteenth century, the French aristocracy became so hot they appointed a door fan to provide air to the throne, which was under threat from the English.

The door fan's biggest fan was a young woman named Joan who designed a label for it which read 'Made in Orleans'. She was part of the Arc family, an influential circle that signed and co-signed her essay, written in support of the door fan but also as a criticism of cat lovers in the area.

Church leaders at the time, however, were cat-a-holics who considered that Joan had gone off on a tangent and that her opinion was hearsay and so they stretched her on the rack before burning her at the stake for her essay.

This gave rise to the saying 'gone to rack and Rouen.'

RENE DESCARTES

Noticing that peasants got awfully wet when caught in showers of precipitation, he patented the design of the covered wagon and quickly became known to all as Rainy Day Cart.

He suffered from a fear of washing and, not caring what others thought, famously declared 'I stink therefore I hum'.

This led firstly to a phenomenon called the cordon blur, a fog which emanated from him in all directions warning people of the smell.

Loneliness and having to communicate by megaphone forced him to invent Perfume which he marketed under the 'Body Eau de' brand.

LOUIS XIV (LOUIS QUATORZE)

Louis was the first carthorse to rule France and sired Louis XV, who became the first royal winner of the Prix de L' Arc de Triomphe.

Another descendant was Louis XVI, who lost by a head in the race a few years later after taking a tumbrel on the final bend.

Carthorse was the first monarch to apply an anagram to his name after doing orchestra-1 manoeuvres in the dark one night. He was also the first one-eyed ruler in Europe and became known as Louis sole eye or the Sun King after developing the sun-king garden which became a joke at the time in court and thus gained the name 'ha-ha'.

Louis should not be confused with the famous birdman, Al Catraz, who was half auk, half kestrel and instigated the famous newspaper headline 'Auk-Kestrel Man Hoovers in the Dark' after being reported to the governor when his vacuum cleaner disturbed neighbouring prisoners.

MAXIMILIEN DE ROBESPIERRE.

Noticing the success of the Rainy Day Cart, Robespierre founded the most prestigious fashion house of the day and started a revolution in the sale of raincoats.

He opened 'Macs a Million' in 1789 which attracted storming reviews in 'Bastille' that had people losing their heads in the rush to be the first in Choppers Walk.

Based on his initial success, he launched 'Robes by Pierre' and 'Pierre Cardigans' which over time was shortened to Cardin.

Although the French were revolting at the time his dress sense paved the way for the development of the style for which the French of today are renowned.

He also invented the Bee-hive hair style (which re-emerged in the 1950s) and it was noticeable that thousands, particularly in the Aristocracy, were bee-headed at the time.

NAPOLEON BONAPARTE

So much has been written about perhaps the most famous Frenchman never to win the Tour de France that this short resume will confine itself to the private man, the face that France never saw.

As a child he suffered with an inferiority complex which he overcame by insisting that he could perform any task given him.

Nicknamed 'Course I can' by his schoolmates he developed the nasty habit of keeping his hand on the bony part of his anatomy and had no compunction in agreeing to being painted in this pose on a number of occasions.

He also developed a fixation with removing his trousers at twelve minutes past six every evening, leaving them on the back of a dining chair, instead of hanging them up in the wardrobe, a fact recorded for posterity by Tchaikovsky in his 18.12 over chair.

During his invasion of Russia he reputedly struck up a platonic relationship with the tennis player Marat Safin, which he kept secret until his dying day. That is except for the famously reported occasion when he told the Empress why he could not join her for a boudoir biscuit with the words 'Not tonight Jo, Safin's on the telly'.

Evidence to this effect was hinted at by the renowned historian, Dan Brown, who, in breaking The Napoleonic Code discovered that he had suffered with tennis elba between 1814 and 1815.

He spent his final days on the island of St Helena where he abandoned tennis for rugby and wrote his famous treatise on loneliness, Helena Rugby, later adapted by The Beatles.

HENRI DE TOULOUSE-LAUTREC

Henri was one of a group of painters in Paris who became famous for their portraits of Frenchmen impersonating wooden posts.

Henri's parents were first cousins and expert players of *Incest* advertised by its manufacturer as 'a game for all the family'.

Henri's parents ignored the Government health warning which was stamped on the box and continued to play without taking the recommended precautions and as a result little Henri remained little Henri for life. In later life he became an avid fan of Star Trek and as the ears went on became known as Le Trekkie.

JACQUES ANQUETIL

A Frenchman is never happier than when he is on his bike and Jacques was no exception, winning the Tour of France five times on his drop handlebar, three speed Derailleur, getting to wear the coveted Yellow jumper as he cycled round Paris on the final day.

No one really knows his true surname, although he carried with him a picture of the man thought to be his father taking part in the first ever bicycle race in France.

Anquetil was a nickname given to him because of two dissimilar traits.

First of all he could never lose the smell of a small dabbling duck which had pervaded his personage since child hood.

The other, inherited from his father was his annoying habit of having a loud horn fitted to the handlebars of his cycle which he would honk furiously if anyone held him up until they got the message and moved over.

JACQUES ANQUETIL SNR

AGM: OPU STEERING COMMITTEE: PHILOSOPHY, PSYCHOLOGY AND PSYCHIATRY

Minutes:

A one minute silence was observed in memory of Eddie Puss, the Psychology Department's pet cat, who died after getting its head caught in the newly fitted Entrechat.

1

A statement on the recently opened Eddie Puss Complex was well received. The departmental sculptor, Jo, cast a bronze effigy which now stands at the entrance to the eclectic mix of shops, exhibition halls and cafes. One faculty head commented that on the opening day he had bought his wife a Freudian slip in the lingerie shop but she had returned it because she felt it was too Jung for her.

2

Frau Jung, a mountain of a woman if read from the back, was introduced as the new faculty head of Psychology and Psychiatry. A keen golfer, she suggested the reintroduction of the transatlantic tournament, based on the Ryder Cup format, with fearsomes in the morning and foibles in the afternoon. Match play singles would not be considered after the debacle of the last 'Bats at the Belfry Cup' when the American Captain, 'Crazy' Pavin set fire to the trousers of Colin Montgomerie, apparently at the request of a Miss Thurman. Montezuma's Revenge was duly noted, although the motive remains unknown.

3

Agreed that a seminar would be held to discuss various Philosophy department issues including:

Sartre's theory of a 50p price fixing on any product to come out of the rear end of a chicken ... noted under 'Eggs is ten shillings-ism'... and its relationship to 'Baconian Rasher-nalism'. Frau Jung, who has developed a Yorkshire accent, commented 'Alpen as like' as a possible alternative.[9]

4

Talk of Muesli led to the noting of the success story of the feline veterinary service that had opened in the complex. The practice is run by Kitty, a Maoist and a firm believer in the doctoring of the cat.

---

[9] ''Appen as like' is a popular Yorkshire saying

Having travelled the world she has divided up her premises into geographical regions to coincide with the cats' condition.

Those arriving with a heavy cold are put into Mogadishu but those with tight chests are normally confined to Qatar. Those needing isolation go to Catalonia, those unfortunates who have been plucked from being flushed down the toilet by uncaring owners go into Kathmandu, and those who sadly pass on may be laid to rest in Khartoum. It's not all doom and gloom however, because, on a more pleasant note, Kitty is organising a 'rear of the year' competition for all her patients, the prize for which is guaranteed to be a massive Catastrophe.

5

A discussion on the merits of old and new texts available at the bookshop then followed.

Heidegger's 'Introduction to Philosophy for Australians' is attracting interest. So too is Spinoza's text on revolving noses for clowns, while Savonarola continues to offer quality cars at reasonable prices.

Jung's theory of the collective unconscious has been taken up by the Glasgow City Ambulance Service who now pick up at midnight on a regular basis in the city centre.

I'm manual Kant's articles on refusing to accept mechanical devices are also under discussion and people are beginning to realise that Foucault knew very little.

6

The meeting closed with a visit to the complex cafe where free Hobbes-Nobs were served to ladies who had been practising Schopenhauer's theory that sixty minutes exactly is the period of time for which females are at their most effective in terms of the purchasing of articles.

COMING TO A CINEMA NEAR YOU

'FEEL THE HAIRS ON YOUR HEAD BRISTLE WITH FEAR'

If it's in a quack

Not a coo or cluck

You can't get rid of

The Barber Duck

First hear a rumble

Reminiscent of drums

But it's just his tummy

Eager for crumbs

A lonely single mother, a young boy who refuses to leave the house to have his hair cut, an old yellow paged book, found on top of a wardrobe, which you can't get rid of—the yellow pages, not the wardrobe.

Mr Barber Duck: Mobile Hairdresser.

Don't let him in

Whatever you do

If it's too late

Go hide in the Loo

He'll snip at the ends

At the curls and the loops

All will seem well

Then you'll hear

'Quack Quack, OOPS!

He'll eat all the bread

That you saved for your dinner

And meantime your son

Starts to look like Yul Brynner

So if you hear a quack

Not a coo, nor a cluck

As he walks past the window

Remember to DUCK

BARBER!

DUCK, DUCK! DUCK!

THE OPU FRENCH POCKET DICTIONARY

A MUST FOR THE TRAVELLER WHO NEEDS

ONLY A FEW WORDS TO GET BY

MULTIPLE OPTIONS AVAILABLE WITH SOME WORDS

A

A la minute

Frighten my pet aquatic amphibian

A la mode

Poem about a young sheep

Lawn miraculously cut overnight (Religious conditions apply)

To have fought to the death after having been surrounded by
Mexican soldiers in an old church e.g. to have been Alamo-ed

ALAMO-ED

Abattoir

Short-handed lisping Swedish tribute band, best known for version of 'I had a Dweam'

Adieu

Compulsory tipping instruction on French restaurant bill

Ammoniac

A Tibetan beast of burden that never stops complaining about the loads it has to carry. Some end up in Celery-Yak

Apostrophe

Award presented to 'French Mailman of the Year'

Art deco

An unauthorised peek at a new gallery show

Au pair

Irish twins

B

Belle Époque

Fatty part of a pig popular in Asian cuisine

Billet doux

British Airways cabin staff party

Bonhomie

Title of autobiography of U2 lead singer

Boutique

To show one's disapproval for a particular type of wood

C - M

Cafe au lait

Bistro that uses red tablecloths positioned with a flourish, by bullish gaudily dressed waiters.

Candide

Act of heroism performed at French film festival

Cause celebre

Remnants of apples eaten by famous celebrities of the day e.g. Uruguayan footballer, Luis Suarez

C'est la vie

Put one's toilet up for sale

Charge d'affaires

Alimony: usually all your money

Concierge

Give the impression that one has an overwhelming desire to join the navy

Concordat

Distinctive pointed cap worn by air crew on first supersonic transatlantic flight

Corps de Ballet

Body for burial at end of 'The Dying Swan'

Crème Brule

A cup of tea with milk at the crematorium café

Crème fraise

Newly urn'd ashes

Debut

French reaction to team setback

Déjà vu

Cinema chain showing films you think you may have seen before

Esprit de corps

Holy Ghost

Film noir

Biblical epic with Russell Crowe in title role

Laissez- faire

Cost for taking famous Hollywood dog on a bus

Lingerie

Hanging about in women's underwear

Litterateur

Man who can't stop himself picking up paper in the street

Motif

Verbal request to dentist to replace missing items on denture plate

N-P

N'est-ce pas

Infestation found in Frenchmen's

trousers.

Outre

Particularly big Frenchman's nose (The nose not the Frenchman)

Pain au Chocolat

A choco-colic

Pain au raisins

French antipathy with having to explain their actions

Papier-mâché

Grandfather's liquidised meals

Pas de deux

Father of twins

Pastiche

Frenchman's idea of a joke is to ridicule gourmet Cornish lunchtime snack

Patois

Death sentence placed by Pope on Irish author for writing in a terrible accent

Pince-nez

Refuse to put on one's trousers. Popular in Shakespearean plays or impressions of Frankie Howard [10]

Portmanteau

Tugboat skipper

---

[10] Frankie Howard was a British comedian with a unique turn of phrase

Précis

Short but expensive

Q-S

Quai d'Orsay

Voice activated home entry device

Sabotage

Plot to blow up a Belgian shoe

Saboteur

A connoisseur of Saab motor cars

Sombre

Three quarters of a Mexican hat

Sommelier

More 'niffy' than normal

T-Z

Tete-a-tete

A collection of potato art at a foremost London gallery

Tout de suite

Mozart composition for the kazoo

Vinaigrette

A young eagle poached in **a** wine sauce

Zut alors.

The Turin Shroud

BREAKING NEWS

London

History made as first ever motion passed during an AGM of National Society of Sufferers from Constipation. Israeli delegate requests return of pre-paid membership for forthcoming year.

London

The Commission for Racial Equality wishes it to be known that The Race Relations Board no longer exists. This follows complaints addressed to the old board by senior citizens in Liverpool regarding a recent Sports Day at a local primary school. Most complaints were made with regard to the 100m sprint where aunties were forced to compete against uncles. One grandfather in the mixed relations egg and spoon race stopped at the halfway point for a picnic, not having been informed of the rules regarding the eating of the equipment supplied.

Paris

Canadian is first to be eliminated in the annual 'Guess Which Country the Contestant Wearing a Wig Represents' competition after judging panel cannot fail to notice Maple Leaf Syrup on his head[11]

Miami

Huge search and rescue operation eventually called off after unattended Lilo found floating in strong currents off the Miami coast. Lionel Lopez said "Jennifer will kill me when she finds out that I went swimming immediately after a rather heavy lunch."

Los Angeles

R2D2 and Declan MacManus announce signing of contract to make 4 new 'A Bot and Costello' films.

Zurich

---

[11] 'Syrup' is Cockney rhyming slang for 'wig'

Sepp Blatter allegedly resigns from FIFA amidst rumours of powerful new job on the horizon. A copy of Jules Verne's '20,000 Leagues under the Sea' later found in his office.

Dublin

Irish Government announces amalgamation of Vasectomy and Hip Replacement Services. Video explaining the rationale has U2 front man singing new theme for the service: 'Nick knack, Paddy whack, Give the dog a bone, this old man goes limping home'

Isle of Wight

A man is today recovering after being airlifted from the 'Gibraltar to Llanfairpwllgwyngyllgogerychwyrndrobwllllantysiliogogogoch Ferry' which had run aground in heavy seas and is not now expected to be refloated for at least two days. The man paid £5000 for the service which guaranteed he would make a vital business meeting taking place tomorrow. When interviewed he admitted that he could ill afford the money but with the impending meeting he found himself stuck between a rock and a hard place.

London

'Pounded Land' bargain retail group announces release of a musical Sat. Nav. for just £1. Very useful for those wishing to bypass Lancaster and /or Cornwall –Plays 'Pass the Duchie on the left/right hand side' or if road works are being managed by a 'Stop/Go' lollipop sign wielding duo - Plays 'On the road to Mandalay'.

BOOKS YOU THOUGHT YOU KNEW

Books with familiar sounding titles aimed at drawing the attention of potential buyers are hitting the High Street on a daily basis. The following are all examples of the new 'genre':

You may treat it as a quiz if you wish. Just cover the page with a sliding piece of paper or act as question master.

"George and Lenny leave the USA during the depression to go plate painting in Germany but discover all too quickly that it's not all it's been cracked up to be."

Of Meissen Men

"Bimbo waitress distracts drinkers during the Munich Beer Festival as part of a scam to serve short measures in large steins while charging full price."

Low Litre

"Didn't he do well for all those years with the BBC, but now that he's been retired, all he does is drone on and on about the new country style cooking range that he's had installed in his kitchen. Bruce basically runs through the full spec for the cooker, leaving the reader aghast and, by the end, totally browned off."

The Forsyth's Aga

The first of its author's novels to be published it tells the story of a French priest tending to the spiritual needs of a group of aircraft maintenance men during the Napoleonic wars.

North Hanger Abbé

Fog delayed in Port-au-Prince after being put in a trance on the island, a gambler takes on the biggest challenge ever without his suitcase but fortunately not without his passport too.

Around the World in a Haiti Daze

Political hypocrisy at its worst in this factual account of a Middle Eastern leisure break taken by the head man of the 2014 Scottish drive for Independence. Sounds fishy and it is.

Salmond, Fishing in the Yemen

An account of the events surrounding the appearance of twins in a Southern States courtroom charged with doing away with a sarcastic pet parrot that had been making their lives a misery.

Two Kill a Mocking Bird

In an ironic classic, a hardy author rewrites his treatise on Latvian bog snorkelling after seeing the slobbery mess made by his dog of his original manuscript. Dog's teeth are removed as a precautionary measure for the future to ensure that there can be no recurrence of his devastating action.

Chewed The Obscure.

A tale of the meagre lachrymose drops of Deputy Dawg's faithful companion after his exposure to 'Dat onion I was given'.

The Three Muskie Tears

On a Mediterranean island in WWII, two teams of domestic pets play a football tournament with the winning team getting to go home to their owners. But someone keeps moving the goalposts

Cats 22

OPU CLASSICS

ASSOCIATION FOOTBALL-THE EARLY YEARS

ANCIENT GREECE

Game invented by Socrates who devises the name 'Association Football' in the absence of any other suggestions from the cleverest men in Athens.

Cynics denounce the game as Pi in the Sky but open negotiations with GT to share television coverage.

Each team is allocated one God. Some import Romans from Ceres A.

Sponsorship is shared between Nike (Boots) and King Priamark (Kit)

Complaints received about 'off the peg' kit at King Priamark where small size shorts are found on same hanger as XXL shirts.

First ever 100 drachma transfer is paid for Alf, a Centaur forward who's a good lad with a hell of a hoof on him (4 to be precise).

Alf is managed by his brother, Alf, a Centaury bright star of the future. His agency was 4.37 light years from the Sun, so got little publicity in his early days,

He spots and signs Robin Van Perseus playing with Ajax at Troy where he stars in the defeat of the Gorge-ons,

Helen, the Delia Smith of the day, owns the Gorge-ons who give her the nickname, "The Face that lunched 1000 chips".

They are managed by Gianfranco Zola who marries Medusa and persuades Helen to drop the E from their name.

Rival fans now carry banners with the message 'Gorgon's Zola Stinks'

Mirror Scoop; Medusa loses her head in a scuffle with Van Perseus and is banned for life after turning to stone the face of Van Perseus' old boss, David Moyes.

Helen leaves Zola and goes to Paris where the cold forces her to wear many layers of clothes.

Luckily she remembers to take her Trojan clothes horse with her which has built in compartments for 'surprise surprise' packages run by Scylla.

Agent system begins and clubs warned "Beware of Greeks bearing gifts."

All kids now aspire to be a Centaur forward but few have the required constitution of a horse.

Blythe Spartans, an elite fighting force, with a canny ball instinct for defending passes win first Charity Shield against a Corinthian team, far too casual in their approach.

Match sponsored by Hoplite, a non-alcoholic lager brewery.

Disaster follows Blythe Spartans wherever they go in the shape of a Tsun Army.

In Paris, Gianfranco's cousin, Emile, tells Marcel Proust about the 'Geordie' Spartans from Blythe, inspiring him to write "A La Recherché du temps Pardew", a history of their much maligned manager.

First coach and trainer of National team is Pythagoras who develops midfield triangle system.

First injuries occur when ancestor of Marty Pellow develops fungal growth on his patellae after playing in damp conditions.

De-moss the Knees, a cold cream, is invented to treat Pellowpy Knees sufferers when it's Wet, Wet, Wet.

Achilles thrown out of National squad for not a-tendon training and becomes first player transferred overseas when Ajax, now living in Amsterdam, pays 300 Billion drachma for him. (Early signs of Greek inflation)

Team, Ajax of Amsterdam created to deter-gents from fouling the gutters and wetting the Press.

They continue to affect Greek football by taking Theseus on loan after his amazing feats on a minor tour of Crete.

Greek league delta fatal blow when Zeno leaves Stoic City to replace Hera between the Styx in the Underground XI.

Hera says she will be sorry to go as she loved to hear the chant of the dead, killed by the Tsun Army, who ask for quiet before wailing SH Hera, SH Hera.

Greek league folds when councils decide to tarmac all grounds.

Greek commentator, Demis Woolstenhome, overseeing the final steam rolling of the tarmac says "Some people are on the pitch. They think it's all over. It is now."

Appendices: Greek for 'writers' cramp'

Traits of the teams and their gods

Cyclops: Always had one eye on the clock

The Fates: accepted decisions without argument (unlike The Furies)

The Hedonists: good in the air, a pleasure to watch

Charon: most popular name for the WAGS of the league

The Lampades: Father and Son who played for the torch bearers of the underworld

The Harpies: forever complaining about bad refereeing decisions

Scylla: famed for going on blind dates with footballers. Had links with Bundesliga queen Lorra Lorra lie

The Sirens: used to end matches and warn when the Tsun Army was on the way

Artemis: scored the most open goals in League history.

Argo-noughts: lowest scorers in the League's history

Castor and Pollux: inventors of the iron jock strap

Midas: first football pools king

Sisyphus: speaks for himself

And how much did a Grecian earn? Pots

PLAY

THE SECOND LINE GAME

SELECT A FAMOUS FIRST LINE FROM A BOOK

AND WRITE THE SECOND YOURSELF

EG

"CALL ME ISHMAEL"

"BUT REMEMBER MA, OUR SURNAME IS FISHMAIL"

THE OLD PUN UNIVERSITY ART EXHIBITION

IDENTIFY THE FAMOUS ARTISTS FROM THEIR FIRST

SKETCHES WHICH WERE INTENDED TO MAKE THEIR

NAMES KNOWN TO THE PUBLIC

WW1 BOMB CRATER (A SAFE PLACE TO HIDE)

ANDY WAR HOLE

EYELID-LESS LIZARD LEARNS TO DRIVE

L GECK0

A SOOTHING BALM FOR A BEACH-SORE BACKSIDE

SAND RAW BOTTY JELLY

RENT A DODGY GERMAN WASHING MACHINE.

HIRE OMINOUS BOSCH

SCOTSMAN HOLDS ON FOR DEAR LIFE

CANNA LET GO

OLD FRENCH FRANCS ATTACKED BY THE CAT.

CLAWED MONEY

MARSUPIAL SAINTS CHECK THEIR RUBBISH

CONTAINERS.

PETER PAUL 'ROO BINS

AN ITALIAN GREENGROCER'S VAN

CARRY VEGGIO

TOILET AT THE US MASTERS

AUGUSTA'S JOHN

BREAKING NEWS

New York

Experimental stage version of 'Gone with the Wind' closes as offensive shouting match between the two actors sharing the lead role brings chaos to matinee performance. Director says," I warned the producers that two Rhetts on the stage wouldn't work".

Calcutta

Traditional father/son relationships under strain are again in the news as arranged marriage called off when father discovers son at an all-male dinner and dance. Reported by restaurant magazine 'Balti-More News' with headline 'Poppadum Founded at Chapatti'

New York

'Rapping Christmas Presents Neatly' by Jay-Z goes straight into Best Sellers handicrafts section at Number one.

Dublin

2014 Best Seller under 'Hobbies and Pastimes' remains 'River Dancing and Stamp Collecting' by Michael Philately.

Athens

Scientists report that following initial experiments induced by reading 'OPU' feature on 'Soccer in the Ancient Greek World', the cloning of a mythical Greek entity and a Basil Brush look-alike has just resulted in the 'birth' of the 20th Centaury Fox. Leader of team says 'It is of Paramount importance that we get this filmed as soon as possible'. RK Ologists who discovered the DNA of centaur in Columbia agree that it is of Universal significance. MGM put in official complaint that they are not included in pathetic joke.

Cardiff

New Zealand Rugby Union team in court accused of breaching Press Regulations. Captain said "We had no idea when we phoned the Welsh team hotel at 3am that telephone Hakas were frowned upon here."

London

Bricklayers taken to task at site of a new Finishing School when secretary appears to tell them it's rude to point

Swansea

Welshman and Japanese tourist engage in longest ever recorded conversation at cross purposes. Lloyd Lewis said 'I was talking about the merits of 'Heart of Glass' by Blondie but it appears that the Welshman thought I was eulogising on the central grasslands of Burundi'

Harvard

Chaos ensues at conference on the Monroe Doctrine as one half of the room supports America's 1823 warning to Europe to stay out of North and Latin American affairs, while the other half disputes the findings of post mortem on Hollywood star found dead in motel room in 1962. Organisers blame use of predictive text in issuing invitations.

NEW HISTORY FROM THE OPU

INDONESIA AUGUST 1883

On a pre-season tour of Indonesia, Newcastle United FC organise first ever away package for their fans.

Cracker Tours of Newcastle arrange for the city's famous 'Toon Army' to accompany the players on a mission to bring the game to developing nations and return with the photographs.

The now famed supporters, who could barely understand one another's Geordie accents never mind a foreign language, became the victims of the first ever onomatopoeia-ic disaster when, unable to decipher local news reports of volcanic activity in the area, believed the indigenous population was fleeing in the face of themselves. One hour later the 'Toon Army' met a Tsunami face on and came off the worse.

Cracker Tours never ran any further trips east of Java.

BOMBAY 1945

Harry Corbett, the doyen of glove puppet entertainment was in India during the war, and happened to become involved in a Hindu funeral where he witnessed the traditional ritual known as Suttee which involved the grieving widow throwing herself onto her husband's funeral pyre to join him in the thereafter.

After the flames had subsided and the mourners had toasted their marshmallows, Harry met two workers who were charged with clearing up after the event. The foreman spoke very quietly into the ear of the other, whose name was IzzyWizzy, suggesting that they get busy so that they could finish early. After clearing up they drove off in their van emblazoned with the company name: Dizzy and Izzy Wizzy: Cleaners to the Bereaved, You Suttee: We Sweep.

Anyway, apparently it was the bus driver on the way back to the hotel who suggested that Harry take up a career as a straight-man to a pair of naughty glove puppets, one of whom could be a cute bear named Sooty and the other a dog named Sweep.

Just think, if Harry had taken a taxi home he may never have come up with the idea.

PLAY 'JOIN THE TITLE' GAME

SELECT YOUR CATEGORY; FILMS, BOOKS, SONGS ETC AND THEN ATTEMPT TO MAKE THE LONGEST OR MOST AMUSING SENTENCE BY JOINING TOGETHER VALID TITLES. ALLOW ADDITIONAL PUNCTUATION WITHOUT PENALTY.

Suggestions:

 "Old Yeller" "Brokeback Mountain" "Digby, the Biggest Dog in the World"

"If" "My Left Foot" "Can. Can" "Da's Boot" "Bend it like Beckham?"

THE OPU ARCHIVE OF QUOTES,

'

"I don't mind dying but I hate to leave my friend's behind"

Thought to be the last words of Liberal Archie

"Are you sitting uncomfortably? Then I'll begin"

Torquemada (introducing Spanish version of BBC Radio's 'Listen with Mother')

"There are lice, damned lice and stick insects"

Samuel Longhorn Clements, spokesman for the Texan Cattleman's Club

"Genies are ninety nine percent imagination and one percent perspiration"

Anonymous, but thought to be a lad in a pantomime

"There's many a Twix `tween cup and lip"

Motto of the Obesity society

"How do I love thee? Let me count the ways"

Elizabeth Barrett Browning reading about her use of the Kama Sutra in 'Sonnets from the Portuguese'

"I will arise and go now, and go to Innis, free"

W. B. Yeats poem about his fare dodging on country buses, unaware that a Tickety-Boo exponent was to be his conductor that day.

'Neither a borrower nor a lender be'

Shakespeare's opposition to the Elizabethan public library service

'Men often make passes at girls with big arses'

Neater Loos (Fashion Magazine)

"Oi just com ober on the loose, Titania, but got sunk by a German U-boat on the way''

'I 'a go to hotello, but the more of Venice I see, the less I like it'

2 original quotes from the unused draft for Shakespeare's 'Comedies of Eire'

'There's a breathless hush, it's so close tonight

Ten left in and the dance to win

And it's not for the sake of a ribboned coat

Nor the pair of trousers to match I bought...'

Sir Henry Newbolt's poem on 'Strictly Come Dancing', and the 'Vital Lambada'

'Friends, Romans, Countrymen,

Lend me your ears.

I come to Bury...'

Brutus opening his speech to the people of a Lancashire town while on diplomatic service

FINALE

We end Volume I with a mixed bag of one-liners

If eating in a restaurant remember:

 Chicken Dopiaza what you wear at Easter bonnet parades

Bombay duck is a warning sign on a B42 Bomber's fuselage

Haute Cuisine is not French Porridge but the asking and answering of questions on the subject of the oat.

Vindaloo is not an Indian restaurant house wine

Antipasto is not a formicary

If stuck on a ship in the Bay of Biscay as the wind freshens and the black clouds gather, retire to your cabin with a litre of cut price 'Old Tawny' and say "Ah well, any port in a storm,"

Until Volume II

COMING SOON: VOLUME II

The 2015 Hannibal Lecture on Cereal killers in old Carthage.

Premiere of new Frog Hoppera, 'The Kermitments'

Was Bach's 'Air on a G String' originally banned for its dim innuendo?

What part did Jack Hughes play in the 'Dreyfus' affair?

Why did Scarlett O'Hara change her name to Frank Lee?

If the EU required a Minister for Geometry would it try Angela Merkel?

Is a Chicken Ecclestone curry a little burny in the mouth?

Did footballers in the French Foreign Legion practice Kepi-Uppy in the desert?

Do other people find residents of the Vietnamese capital really Hanoi-ing?

Why did Edith Pilaf lead the opposition to The Rug rats on French TV and was she involved in the plot to bury Arnie?

Was Jacques Tati really scruffy?

Is a coup pigeon English?

Was there ever a French cannibal named 'Al who ate her?'

Printed in Great Britain
by Amazon